BRIGHT · SPARK

We can build...

Rosie Dalzell

Photographs: Zul Mukhida

Series Consultant: Sue Dale Tunnicliffe

Geddes+ Grosset

First published in hardback 1991
Copyright © Cherrytree Press Ltd 1991 and
Touchstone Publishing Ltd 1991

This paperback edition first published 1991 by
Geddes & Grosset Ltd
David Dale House
New Lanark, ML11 9DJ

ISBN 1 85534 448 3

Printed and bound by
Proost N.V., Turnhout, Belgium

Contents

Projects

Words

Difficult words are explained on p. 26.

Check

Before you start any project, check to see if there is a safety note (marked !) in the text. This means you need an adult to help you.

Topple testing

Stacey is slowly tilting her board. Which container will fall over next? Stacey has made some guesses with paper shapes. Has she guessed right?

Why don't you test some empty plastic pots and bottles in the same way? A starting line of plasticine will stop them sliding. Make paper shape guesses.

Dominic is going to test an empty bottle and one with some sand in the bottom. Which one will topple first?

◄Tall trees have huge roots underground to keep them stable.

Tower engineering

Leila and Laurie are playing a game to see who can build the taller tower. Try this game with a friend.

You each begin with the same number of bottles and packets. Your tower must stay up when you blow it gently, so use as many stable shapes as you can.

Do you think Leila's tower will stay up when she blows it? Which tower has a broad base?

▶ **The Eiffel Tower has a broad base cemented into heavy** foundations **under the ground to make it stable.**

Patterns in brick

Look for different brick patterns on walls near your home. You will be surprised how many there are. Try copying them with interlocking bricks.

Some arrangements of bricks are stronger than others. Ruth is testing her walls by pushing them. Which wall is weaker? What other tests could she use?

Invent some brick patterns of your own and make drawings to record your patterns.

◄The arrangement of these bricks is strong. The pattern of coloured bricks is for decoration.

Great girders

Leila is using toy people to test some paper **girders**. The sheets of green paper are all the same size, but she has folded them differently.

You can see which is the stronger girder on her house in the picture. What about the other ones? Fold some sheets of paper and test them, with a flat piece, in the same way.

Build some paper structures with your strongest girders.

►**Will these H-shaped girders make a stronger roof than a flat sheet of metal?**

Balancing bridges

Try to build a tower of bricks that leans out. Where do you have to add extra bricks to stop it falling over?

If you bring two of your towers together, as Dominic has, they can make a bridge. Will it fall down when Dominic puts the blue brick on?

Can you build a bridge big enough to let one of your boats through?

◄The beams of the Forth rail bridge stretch across the river. The weight each side of the pillars has to balance, like your brick bridges.

Supporting arches

Nicky wanted his paper road to carry cars over the railway line. First he built two brick pillars and laid his road on top to make a flat bridge. Try making a bridge like this and see what happens.

Now Nicky is using some more paper to make his bridge stronger. Can you see what he's doing?

How many cars will this bridge hold? Make a paper arch bridge with bricks or books and find out.

▶ **The stones in the arches of this bridge are wedged snugly together. They push against each other to carry the load on top.**

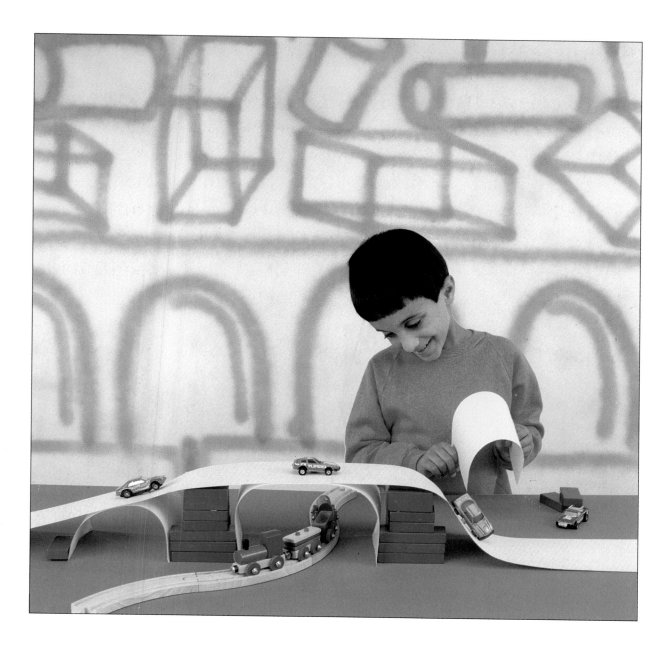

Strong shapes

Engineers need to know how to join beams together to make a strong, firm framework. You can work out how they do it using some strips of card, as Ruth has done.

Punch a hole at each end of the strips. Join them together with paper fasteners. Make a shape with three sides, then four, five, six, seven . . .

Which shapes bend easily? Which are rigid and strong?

◄The Pompidou Centre in Paris is held up on the outside by a huge frame of steel beams, joined in a criss-cross pattern of triangles.

Super straws

Nicky is designing things for a playground. His models are made from plastic straws and modelling clay.

Some of the structures wobbled to begin with. Can you see how he solved this problem?

Build yourself a model climbing frame that you would like to play on. Remember to use strong shapes and, if possible, a wide base.

! **Keep the clay off the carpet – and your clothes.**

►**The person who designed this climbing frame may have made a model first, just as you have done.**

18

Furniture fun

Look what James and Bronwyn have built with newspaper and sticky tape! Newspaper is thin and floppy, but see what happens when you roll it into a tube.

Try taping a bundle of tubes together. Will it hold the weight of your teddy? Bronwyn has made a table by joining her tubes in shapes that make them stronger.

See what you can build with newspaper tubes.

◄Can you see which pieces of furniture are made from steel tubes? They are light and strong, like your newspaper furniture.

21

Crazy concrete

Try making **concrete** out of sand, small stones and **cement**. Ruth put in three spoons of sand for every one of gravel and one of **plaster of Paris**. Leila is adding water.

When it is a creamy paste, they can pour it into moulds. It will take a week to set well.

Put strips of wire or straw into some of your moulds. Which mixture makes the strongest concrete?

! **Put left-over concrete in the bin, not down the sink.**

▶ **Here concrete is being mixed and poured into a wooden frame to shape it into pavement** foundations.

Tent technology

Can you make your own den with **bamboo** canes and an old sheet or rug? You will need some string and clothes pegs too. Practise your strongest knots.

Stacey's den stays up well. Can you see why? Dominic is going to try a different idea for his den, but he will still use strong shapes and a broad base, as Stacey has done.

Why not make a den with a friend and have a party?

! **Be careful not to poke a bamboo stick in your eye.**

◀ Tents are the best sort of home for people on the move, especially in warm countries.

Words to remember

Bamboo The dried stems of giant tropical grasses, hollow inside.

Beam Long, straight piece, usually of wood, metal or concrete. A beam bridge has flat beams supported on pillars.

Cement Powder which makes a paste with water and hardens as it dries, used to bind together bricks and stones, and to make concrete.

Concrete Man-made building material made of gravel, sand, cement and water.

Foundations Strong base on which something is built.

Girder A beam, usually metal, shaped to make it more rigid, for instance an 'H' shape.

Plaster of Paris White powder (calcium sulphate) that sets after it has been mixed with water.

Books for you

Bricks by Terry Cash (A & C Black)
How Things Are Built by H. Edom (Usborne)
Balancing by Terry Jennings (Oxford)

Books to look at with an adult

Round Buildings, Square Buildings and Buildings that Wiggle Like a Fish by Philip Isaacson (Walker Books)
Forces and Materials and Structures by S.D. Tunnicliffe (Think and Do cards, Basil Blackwell.)

Places to go

The Exploratory, Bristol Old Station, Temple Meads, Bristol BS1 6QU. Experiments and exhibits on structures.
Techniquest, 72 Bute Street, Pier Head, Cardiff CF1 6AA. Design on a computer, then build, a model of a real building.
Stratosphere, 19 Justice Mill Lane, Aberdeen AB1 2EQ. Activities with construction kits, bridges, and more.
Launch Pad, Science Museum, Exhibition Road, London SW7 2DD. Hands-on experiments, especially on bridges.
Ironbridge Gorge Museum, Ironbridge, Telford, Shropshire TF8 7AW. History of the first iron bridge in the world.
The Building Centre, 26 Store Street, London WC1E 7BT.

Sparky ideas

Here are some background facts for adults along with some talking points and more ideas for you to try together.

pp 4–5 Topple testing
• The outcome of Stacey's game depends on the height and the width of the base of the containers, so make sure there is one with a narrow base.
• To be stable, an object needs a broad base (like that of a wine glass or a racing car), or a weighted bottom (low centre of gravity) like a netball post. Trees have both.
• Make a bottom-heavy toy which cannot be pushed over from an egg shell weighted with a lump of plasticine.

pp 6–7 Tower engineering
• Remind the contestants of what they now know about stability.
• Tall buildings, such as skyscrapers, have to stand up to very high winds.
• Some very tall buildings, like the National Westminster Tower in London and the Canadian National Tower in Toronto, are built on a 'raft' foundation. This is a huge, flat slab of concrete under the ground which gives the buildings a broad base and stops them sinking.

pp 8–9 Patterns in brick
• If full-sized interlocking bricks are available, you can build walls big enough to test with a soft ball.
• Look at all the ways bricks are used: for patios, paths, flower beds and chimneys as well as walls.
• When you build a wall with real bricks, the hollows are filled with mortar. As the cement hardens, the bricks are locked together, like the plastic ones.

pp 10–11 Great girders
- Folding gives rigidity to a thin sheet of material, so it can be used to build light, strong structures.
- Look out for folded metal girders on bridges and building sites. Look at corrugated roofs and the shells of limpets and cockles.
- As each girder is tested, keep score together, using similar sized 'weights', and then put the girders in order of strength.

pp 12–13 Balancing bridges
- A beam which sticks out from a support is called a cantilever. The other end is held by something solid or balanced with a weight, as in a cantilever crane.
- A cantilever bridge is built with identical structures on each side of its supports, so they balance each other. The spans of the bridge can be very wide because the forces all weigh down on the supports.

pp 14–15 Supporting arches
- An arch is stronger than a beam because the sides of the bridge (abutments) help to carry the load. The forces pushing down on top of the arch travel through it to the sides and the ground.
- The curve of the arch is often a catenary, the shape a chain makes if you hold an end in each hand. Hold up a string of paper clips and look at the different inverted arch shapes you get as you bring your hands together.
- Experiment with narrow and wide arches to find which shape carries the greatest load.

pp 16–17 Strong shapes
- How can the square be made more rigid by adding just one extra beam? (In fact, by making it into two triangles.)
- Triangle shapes are used in frameworks for bicycles,

roofs, cranes, towers and bridges (see **Tower engineering**, p.6 and **Balancing bridges**, p. 12).

pp 18–19 Super straws
- This is a chance to use ideas from the previous activities to make firm, stable models.
- Get children to use as little modelling clay as possible, so they have to concentrate on making the structure strong.

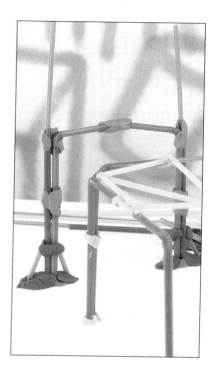

pp 20–21 Furniture fun
- Tubular structures are strong, light and economical of materials. Look for them in playgrounds, tent frames and scaffolding.   See **Great girders**, p. 10 and **Super straws**, p. 18.
- The bones of many animals are often hollow tubes.
- Bundles of tubes are especially strong. Plant stems and tree trunks contain hollow columns of cells, bundled together for support.

pp 22–23 Crazy concrete
- Concrete is a widely used building material today because it is relatively cheap and easy to shape.
- Being a mixture, the proportions of raw materials can be varied, depending on where and how it is to be used. This makes concrete very versatile.
- Concrete is strong when squashed (compressed) but, to make it stronger when bent (under tension), it is reinforced with iron. For increased resistance to impact, short fibres are sometimes added.

pp 24–25 Tent technology
- A triangular pyramid is a particularly strong solid but not very roomy inside. Encourage trying other ideas, using crossed beams for stability. Point out the hollow centres of the bamboos. (See **Furniture fun** notes above.)

Index

Thank you!

The author and publishers would like to thank Greater London Supplies for lending building bricks and Duplo; and the Early Learning Centre for lending building bricks.

We would also like to thank junior technologists Charlie, Ellen Rose, Emily, Francesca, Kate, Laura and Samuel for their work on the projects; and Stacey, Dominic, Leila, Laurie, Ruth, Nicky, James and Bronwyn for appearing in the photographs. Thanks are also due to the teaching staff of St. Luke's Terrace First School, Davigdor Infants School, Stanford First School, St John the Baptist RC First School and Balfour Infants School for their patience and co-operation.

The author would like to thank Hugh and her own children, Thomas, Kate and Harry, for all their help and encouragement.

Picture credits

The projects were all photographed specially by Zul Mukhida. Other pictures were supplied by: ZEFA p. 6 (K. Kerth), 16, 20 (J. Becker), 22 (Starfoto) and 24 (J. Bitsch); Zul Colour Library pp. 4, 8, 10, 12, 14, 18.